Why Do You Walk That Way?

The Story of a Girl with Cerebral Palsy

Amy Cole

Why Do You Walk That Way?
The Story of a Girl with Cerebral Palsy
Amy Cole © 2021

All Bible references taken from the New King James Version.

Softcover ISBN: 978-1-61206-249-5
eBook ISBN: 978-1-61206-243-3

Cover Photo Credit: Sarah Goetter

To purchase this book at quantity discounts, contact Aloha Publishing at alohapublishing@gmail.com

Published by

Printed in the United States of America

To my mom and dad, who always encouraged me to keep writing.
And to my husband, Sean, who never let me
forget my dream of finishing this book.

Contents

Introduction

I began writing this book, because the title wouldn't stop popping into my head: "Why Do You Walk that Way?" This question has followed me my entire life. People both young and old have asked me about the way I walk, and it gives me a unique invitation to tell them a little about myself.

By no means do I speak for everyone with cerebral palsy or with any disability. I am simply one voice among many. But I do believe that what I have to say is important. Speaking about disabilities is the only way that people without disabilities will be able to see into a life they have not experienced. For those with disabilities, these narratives help them understand that they do not struggle alone.

I have often heard it said, "I'm not my disability" or "My disability doesn't define me." And I see where these sentiments are coming from: I would not want someone to hear that I have cerebral palsy and make assumptions about me without getting to know me. Yes, people with disabilities have many different aspects to their lives. And yes, like everyone else, we are diverse and have many different interests and talents. But my disability is not a hobby that I can pick up and put down like poetry or painting. It's an intricate part of my life and it has played a huge role in who I have become. I would not have written this book if I had not been born with this disability.

I've never tried to use my disability as an excuse not to do something if I thought I could do it. Okay, perhaps when it came to junior high P.E. I was more than ready to use it as an excuse. But all joking aside, the feeling of my turn coming next in the rotation during third period volleyball was humbling, because the group had to rotate twice due to the fact that I was unable to serve the ball. In true movie style, there was the cutthroat girl who yelled in front of the whole P.E. class, "Why do we have to rotate twice?" The coach from the sideline yelled, "Knock it off, you know why!" The girl rolled her eyes. She knew why, but she had to make sure everyone else did too. In instances like that, you are given a choice: melt within yourself and forever become the victim, or meet the situation with confidence and realize that a girl who pokes fun at someone disabled has a much deeper problem.

Where did a 13-year-old girl, such as I was, pull such confidence from? Is it the ever elusive "self-esteem" that we're told by the world to somehow muster up in times like that? Self-esteem, if I relied solely on it, would have failed me long ago. I knew that the only way I would be able to walk this life with confidence was by looking outside myself and seeing people for who they really were: individuals struggling with something. Whether that struggle was something I would consider big or small on my own life scale doesn't really matter.

My understanding of this life does not come from just accepting my life circumstances and moving forward. I believe that there is so much more to life than what our finite brains can comprehend. I know that I am not alone on this journey. God has His purposes in everything, though they may seem at times quite mysterious. If after my diagnosis with cerebral palsy my parents had been told that I would become a writer and speak about cerebral palsy and disability in general, would that have wiped away all their tears and calmed all their worries? No. It may have given them some comfort, but they hadn't yet seen it come to fruition. Life is full of unknowns. When you are in the moment, it's hard to see what could possibly lie ahead. I think what most people need to be reminded of in those life-altering moments is that hope, even in things unseen or yet to be, can pull you out of a pit of despair and give more clarity for a future that could possibly surpass anyone's expectations.

If you're wondering a little about my background, I am a wife and mother of two. I am currently a stay at home mom. Before I got to make that move, I taught fourth grade for six years in the public school system. Before that, I taught as a tutor for grades K-12 while I finished my degree. I loved being a teacher for that season in my life.

I was born and raised in southern California and was diagnosed with hemiplegic cerebral palsy at 10 months old. Hemiplegic means it only affects one side of the body. In my case, it's my left side. I have the form they refer to as "spastic" because the muscles on the left side of my body tend to tighten up. After years of physical and occupational therapy, I walk with a slight limp and my left hand has difficulty with fine motor skills. With how cerebral palsy can vary from one individual to the next, mine is considered a mild case of CP.

I moved to Idaho with my family at 18 years old. I had just graduated high school and ended up attending a local university where I graduated with my bachelor's degree in elementary education. I was hired for my first teaching job days before I walked the stage to get my diploma. It was a very exciting time in life.

I worked at a school that was classified as low socio-economic status. I was privileged to be single at the time, although I didn't see it that way then. However, I realized later on it gave me a unique opportunity to dedicate myself almost entirely to my teaching. I hope I taught the 25-30 students not only multiplication skills and reading comprehension, but also helped encourage other life skills like seeing situations from multiple perspectives and having empathy.

My maiden name was Hirsch, and so I named my classroom, "Ms. Hirsch's Haven." I would tell my students at the start of each year that a haven was a safe place, so for those who dealt with difficult life situations outside of school, they could leave their worries at the door and for seven to eight hours a day enter a place where they could learn in peace. It was amazing to see some of the deep exhales some students would release when they heard this. Others were more skeptical at first, questioning whether I would follow through on my promise throughout the year. It was amazing to see the emotional and educational impacts it had on students. I learned that a student who feels safe and unburdened can learn well beyond what was ever expected of them.

I met my husband during my fifth year of teaching. While we were still dating, I brought up a big life dream of mine. While I would never want to give up all the years I had already taught, I'd always wanted to be able to stay home with my children if we were financially capable. His response was that he had always hoped to provide the opportunity for his future wife to have the choice to continue to work or to stay at home if she desired to do that. It was relieving to hear that he was open to both life paths. We got married the next summer and the next year I taught as Mrs. Cole. My classroom name changed to, "Mrs. Cole's Cozy Cabin."

That year I got pregnant with our first daughter. Without any planning at all, it worked out that she would be born in July, so I would be able to finish the entire school year with my students, which I was so happy about. They got to be part of the process, which they loved! During a morning meeting, I revealed to them that I was expecting, and when month five rolled around we got to a math lesson on percentages, I polled the class to see if they thought it was a boy or girl. A parent volunteered to bake cupcakes and secretly fill them with blue or pink. I never had a reveal party with my family because I was so excited I just called them all right after the appointment when I found out I was having a girl. However, the next school day I got to reveal that I was having a girl to my whole class.

As I began to waddle around the last few weeks of school, the teaching chapter of my life was coming to a close. On the last day of school, I was 36 weeks pregnant. Like every year, the last day of school is always filled with so many emotions: excitement for what's ahead and sadness to leave the comfortable and familiar behind. Not all goodbyes are bad—they sometimes allow you to move on to what is next!

The ability to stay home has opened up the door to an idea that previously only seemed like a far off dream. Since I was first able to write, I have always had a journal nearby. I even have a Lisa Frank diary from when I was around 6 years old, when my writing was almost illegible and so giant that some individual letters took up a quarter of page. Writing has always been an amazing outlet for my thoughts. If I can get them down on paper, it has a calming effect. Seeing my thoughts sprawled out in front of me has a way of putting so many ideas in perspective.

And so I was able to write this book. Through it, my hope is that any parent getting a diagnosis for their child knows that it does not have to be life-shattering. It may feel like that in the moment, but that moment will pass. Life will keep going, and that little face is looking to you to see how they should react to such news. Take things one day at a time, one milestone at a time. A child with a disability, just like a child with no disability, will often break through what seem to be unsurpassable odds if they know someone else believes they can do it.

You will notice each chapter concludes with a scripture. These are not just beautiful phrases, but words that have spoken directly to me at pivotal times in my life. They have brought me comfort as well as clarity. I hope that they can do the same for you.

As you read my story, I hope more than anything that it ignites a fire of new hope. I pray that though this life has many twists and turns, you won't let what seems to be a broken bridge keep you from leaping to the other side. The journey that lies ahead can be exciting and full of promise. It may look a bit different than what you had originally planned, but it could be more beautiful than you could ever have imagined!

1

Why Do You Walk That Way?

"Why do you walk that way?" asked a little girl with a Hello Kitty backpack as we stood in a line labeled with a faded yellow six, awaiting our beloved teacher, Mrs. Mayhew. The girl waited impatiently for an answer as she tried to fix the hot pink ribbon falling from her mane of curly brown hair.

"I have cerebral palsy, so it makes my leg tight." I said, the answer rehearsed, repeated often in response to this question.

"Oh. Okay," she said with a smile, her curiosity satisfied for the moment.

She spun back around to stand as straight as possible, hoping for an appreciative comment from our approaching teacher. The squirming line of students began to move forward at Mrs. Mayhew's gentle command. As I stood there waiting to take the first step, I reminded myself that I would try to put my heel down as much as possible as we walked to our third grade classroom. We headed down the cement pathway, past the clay-colored buildings humming with students entering each doorway.

My left foot was not cooperating like I had hoped. Every time I took a step, I felt my toes hit the pavement while my heel remained in midair. Even when I forced it down with as much concentration as possible, it barely grazed the path. Sometimes I wanted to take that heel, sit it down, and have a serious talk with it. I can imagine the conversation going a bit like this:

"Okay heel, I know you like this free ride when I walk, but I need you to help me out here."

"Why?" the heel would say. "The toes are doing a great job."

"Because every time I take a step, I can feel you up in the air."

"Sheesh, okay, okay, I'll try better next time."

The heel and I both knew how unlikely that was.

As I walked toward the classroom, I tried not to pay attention to my hovering heel. The class passed through a number of courtyards, one for each grade level that celebrated a specific group or time period in California state history. So right before we entered our third grade classroom, I always caught sight of the statue of the Native American woman holding her baby standing next to a little adobe hut. I wondered what she would think about all the chattering students who passed her each day.

Mrs. Mayhew's classroom was cozy. My thoughts were quickly consumed by what word Charlotte would spin next on her web in hopes of saving Wilbur. The excitement of the upcoming read-aloud overshadowed any thought of my limp for a time.

The question "Why do you walk that way?" has followed me throughout my life, and I'm quite certain it won't be going anywhere soon. I could never escape the question, nor would I want to now. It has been asked with the bluntness of a child and with the subtly of an adult. I have had to rely on God alone to take the burden of this never ending question from my mind and encourage me to find an answer. Why do I walk this way? Why was I born with cerebral palsy?

> *Cause me to hear Your lovingkindness in the morning,*
> *for in You do I trust; cause me to know the way in which*
> *I should walk, for I lift up my soul to You.*
>
> —PSALM 143:8

2

The Diagnosis

When I was six months old, my mom noticed that I was not tracking her with my eyes in the kitchen. Although I was just a baby at the time, knowing my mom as well as I do, I can picture what it might have looked like. I bet she had a familiar girl movie playing in the background to add a fun ambiance to her daily tasks. She was probably putting away some dishes and popped her head out from the side of the cupboard door in hopes of making me smile. However, it was also a milestone check in. As every mom knows, you are always watching for natural progressions of skills in your babies. Well, when my mom moved to the other side of the kitchen, she noticed my eyes didn't follow her. She immediately stopped the task at hand and tried having me track her finger. My eyes couldn't follow. She was concerned.

When she took me to the pediatrician to voice her worry, he waved it off, saying I was just a bit behind in milestones and she should give it time. She wasn't convinced, but she waited. Then more warning signs appeared. I was army crawling, but my left side was struggling to keep up.

At 10 months, I was finally diagnosed with hemiplegic cerebral palsy. It meant that the muscles on my left side would tend to tighten. The doctor shared the news with my parents, explaining the generalities of what cerebral palsy can consist of and how it may affect my life, such as being placed in a special education classroom. He wasn't sure at the time what I would and wouldn't be able to do. When they got to the car after hearing all the dire possibilities, all they could do was sit in silence. Their little girl who just months before had been thought to be simply behind on growth milestones was now diagnosed with a neurological disorder.

When I eventually did learn to walk at 16 months, my left foot continued to lag behind my right, but I was able to walk without a walking device or aid. I spoke at the typical milestone date of 2 years old without a speech impediment. For a time I spoke with what most characterized as a New York accent, because I often dropped my Rs in certain words. So if you heard me say words like "corner" or "quarter," you might have thought I was visiting from the East. It is actually a family trait, because my mom did that when she was a little girl as well. I grew out of it around nine years old.

Sometimes I wish I could tell my parents at that moment that I would be okay, that this diagnosis was not a life sentence. But they didn't need me to reassure them. They didn't need me to tell them that I would graduate college Magna Cum Laude and become a fourth grade teacher. I didn't need to tell them that I would marry an incredible man and have two precious babies. They looked at me and knew despite my limitations that they would never keep me from trying what I wanted to do. They were always there for me, when I rose past their expectations, or when I fell in an attempt to try something new.

> *For I know the thoughts that I think toward you, says the Lord, thoughts of peace and not of evil, to give you a future and a hope.*
>
> —JEREMIAH 29:11

3

Sirens

To this day, when my mom hears a siren, she says her heart drops and she prays for whoever it might be heading toward. When I was diagnosed with cerebral palsy, the doctor told my parents about the possibility of onset seizures. "She likely won't have seizures if she doesn't have one by her fourth birthday," he said.

And so the wait began.

My parents exhaled deeply when I turned 4 in June.

However, I had my first seizure that following August. I was at my Auntie Stacy's house when it happened.

My mom had just returned from visiting her friend with my older sister, Shannan, and me. My dad had stayed behind to work. The two of them were looking forward to going out on a date and my mom had arranged for Auntie Stacy to babysit Shannan and me. It was their first real date in a while, since they had not wanted to leave me in fear that I would potentially have a seizure when they weren't around. But with my fourth birthday behind us, they finally decided to go out.

I loved my Auntie Stacy's house. It was always filled with familiar voices talking about stories from the past. Auntie Stacy's stories always had a hilarious twist at the end. She is one of the most amazing story tellers. She remembers every detail as if she is still in that very moment and is so animated in her retelling that she could captivate even the most uninterested audience. But when I called her to recount what happened the day of my first seizure, tears replaced her typical laughter.

Auntie Stacy has a big pool in her backyard that any kid would love to swim in, especially on a Southern California August day. Shannan, my three cousins, and I were swimming when Carrie, the youngest of Auntie Stacy's daughters and the one closest to my age, wanted to get out. I was tired as well, so I told Auntie Stacy I wanted to get out too.

While my sister and two older cousins continued to swim, Carrie and I came inside and I snuggled up to Auntie Stacy on the couch, laying my little head on her lap as she played with my hair. A friend of Auntie Stacy's had come over that day, so they kicked back on the couch together, watching the rest of the girls swim around in the pool through the sliding glass door.

Auntie Stacy draped her loving arm over my side and noticed that I had fallen asleep. In my sleep, I began to twitch, what seemed at first to be a typical sleeping twitch. Then it worsened.

"Amy, are you okay?" she gently asked.

No response.

"Amy!" she repeated.

She turned me over in her lap and my eyes were open. The shaking continued. Vomit began to pour out of my mouth and when she picked me up in her arms to take me to the bathroom, I was as straight as a board. She rushed me to the bathroom and held me partly upside down to free my mouth of the leftover vomit.

She yelled to her friend Linda from the bathroom, "Call 911, I think she's having a seizure! She has cerebral palsy, and she's not supposed to have one if she didn't have one by the time she turned 4!"

The ambulance came and I was still incoherent. While my highly concerned 11-year-old sister wanted desperately to come with me, Auntie Stacy was the one to ride with me to the nearest hospital and my sister and cousins stayed behind with Linda.

Auntie Stacy remembers holding my little hand during the ride while the paramedics took over. They moved her to the side multiple times in an effort to take my vitals.

Meanwhile, in a movie theater not far away, my parents were sitting in a movie ironically called *The Doctor*. The movie was interrupted with a quick flick of the lights as the film turned off and an attendant walked in and asked, "Is there a Jeff and Gail Hirsch in the theater?"

My mom's heart dropped and she immediately thought of the pool, where she knew we'd been playing. My parents quickly walked down the theater steps and were beckoned to a lobby pay phone. On the other end was the voice of a firefighter.

"Is this Gail Hirsch?"

"Yes," my mom choked out.

"Your daughter is on the way to the hospital. She has had a seizure."

My mom handed my dad the phone in shock. He took over and got the pertinent details, and then they rushed to the hospital.

While Auntie Stacy stayed with me at the hospital, my Uncle Mitch, who had just got off his shift at the sheriff department, had come to be with her while she waited for my parents to arrive. When my mom arrived in the waiting room, her face was white and her legs were buckling.

My parents were eventually allowed into my room, where I laid still. The doctors had feared that despite Auntie Stacy's quick actions, I still might have aspirated my vomit.

My mom remembers carrying me in her arms, walking me up and down the hospital corridors, trying to fully wake me up, saying my name over and over gently in my ear. I was eventually transported to a larger hospital where I finally became fully conscious.

The only memory I have of that seizure was laying in a child hospital bed that resembled a crib on both sides while holding onto a new stuffed toy my mom had bought me from the gift shop downstairs. Normally I don't like clowns, but this guy was about the size of my hand and had the sweetest expression on his face. I couldn't help but think he was cute. He looked as if he was smiling, but had a single tear falling on his cheek. I asked my mom why she thought he was crying and she responded, "Because he's so happy you're okay." I still have him tucked away in a keepsake box.

Unfortunately, that was not my only seizure. Many would follow, though they wouldn't last forever.

> *My flesh and my heart fail; but God is the strength of my heart and my portion forever.*
>
> —PSALM 73:26

4

Dr. Green's Office

One of the best doctors I've had was Dr. Green. He was my neurologist when I was a little girl. His office was in a big building in downtown Los Angeles. I would look forward to every appointment when I got to see him. One time, during one of our drives to see Dr. Green, my mom told me over the buzz of the freeway, "I just love Dr. Green. I wish we could get him flowers for his office or something."

I sat there in the car thinking about all the funny things Dr. Green had said or done during the past appointments. I can still picture sitting there on the edge of the examination table. He would use the little hammer with the triangular head to check my reflexes. He always acted so surprised when my leg kicked out, and his silly reaction always made me laugh. It is amazing how one doctor could make me feel so happy even though I was in his office for a difficult reason.

When we got to Dr. Green's office that day, things proceeded like they normally had each visit. Dr. Green knocked gently on the door and came in with his beaming face. He grabbed his swirly round doctor chair and pushed his way over to the table with the crunchy white paper, where I waited patiently.

"How are you today, Amy?" he cheerfully asked.

"I'm good," I giggled, hiding a bashful smile.

I leaned over to my mom to whisper a reminder of our conversation in the car. "Mom, we forgot the flowers."

Dr. Green always loved hearing what I had to say. He interrupted my whispering. "What was that, Amy? What are you saying?"

My poor mom, trying to keep the conversation from being misconstrued, said, "Oh, it's just that I was mentioning in the car how much we appreciate you as Amy's doctor and maybe wanted to stop and get you flowers or a plant for your office."

I interjected, "No Mom, that's not what you said, you said you loved Dr. Green and that's why you wanted to get him flowers."

Dr. Green smiled—he appreciated my 5-year-old candidness. My mom shook her head, holding back laughter. I had a habit of doing this type of thing to my mom in Dr. Green's office. I think that's why he would interrupt and ask as often as he did. He knew he was in for a funny story from a 5-year-old with no reservations about giving all the details.

Dr. Green made such a difference in my life. As a child, I was never worried about seeing my neurologist. I hope that any child who has to endure multiple hospital visits gets their own version of Dr. Green.

> *Blessed be the Lord, for He has shown me His kindness in a strong city.*
>
> —Psalm 31:21

5

Standing in Front of the Class

In third grade I got a brace to help with my gait. My mom suggested that I talk to the class about why I was wearing a brace to limit the constant questioning that would surely happen on the playground. At 8 years old, I stood in front of my third grade class with a big plastic brace on my left leg and explained to all the onlooking eyes how it would help me with my walk. I remember standing in front of the whiteboard, the tray edge full of colorful dry erase markers poking my lower back.

"I'm wearing a brace to help stretch out my leg, because my cerebral palsy makes my leg tight."

When I finished my simple explanation, my sweet teacher Mrs. Mayhew asked if anyone had any questions or comments. A little girl in purple raised her hand and said, "I walked pigeon-toed when I was little and had to wear special shoes." After that compassionate comment, the stories came flooding in. Poor Mrs. Mayhew had to reign it in quickly or we wouldn't have learned anything else that day.

That day would be repeated 17 years later, when I was a brand new teacher, standing in front of a fourth grade classroom full of smiling eyes. However, rather than explaining the slight limp from my cerebral palsy to avoid questions, I saw it as an opportunity to teach the students that my limitations couldn't hold me back from what I wanted to accomplish. Whether they had trouble reading or didn't know how to make friends, we were going to learn how to overcome our obstacles together that year.

I gave a similar speech at the beginning of the school year for the next six years. Yet each year, I was still amazed at how the looks of self-doubt in some of those children's eyes would gradually be replaced by a newfound confidence to tackle their own version of a limp, whatever that might be in their life.

> *Be strong and of good courage, do not fear nor be afraid*
> *of them; for the Lord your God, He is the One who goes*
> *with you. He will not leave you nor forsake you.*
> —DEUTERONOMY 31:6

6

The Words on the Bus Go Round and Round

In fourth grade, I sat on the bus waiting to head home after school. Our bus driver, Gloria, grouchily told us to sit on our "buhonkas" so she could start driving. I cautiously adjusted myself on the bus bench, sitting up straight. Gloria was one bus driver you listened to the first time. If the instructions weren't obeyed, she'd often say, "Do I need to come back there and clean house?" I doubt those words would fly these days. All the kids knew she was actually nice, but she just put on a big show to make us believe she was the mean old bus driver.

The next thing I knew, my classmate Cameron plopped down next to me. He was one of the coolest and sweetest kids I knew. Everyone loved him. Every time he saw me, he would give me the biggest smile and I could tell he was truly happy to see me. He was one of those kids with a maturity beyond what anyone would expect from a 10-year-old. He would always sit right next to me and listen to my stories on the way home.

That day when he sat next to me, I was excited to tell him I liked Eric, a silly boy in our class who was always getting in trouble. I asked Cameron, "Do you think he likes me?"

Cameron looked at me so sweetly and said, "Amy, who wouldn't like you?"

Those words have stuck with me ever since. Cameron was one of those kids I spoke to during my speech about my brace in Mrs. Mayhew's class. We were in the same class for both third and fourth grade. When I hung out with him on the playground, he never made me feel self-conscious when I would run and my brace would make a clicking sound every time my foot hit the blacktop. He just saw me, not my brace. The greatest thing about that kid was that he never even realized he had done anything special for me. He was just being a friend.

Your words matter, not only to a little girl with a brace, but to anyone you encounter during your life. Cameron didn't pretend he didn't see my brace. I know he saw it, but he saw it and looked past it to see me. It is that kind of compassion that children and adults alike need to be reminded to practice. Just a couple kind words (that you actually mean) can change a person's life.

The tricky part is to take those opportunities to encourage others when you're given the chance. Don't try to create an opportunity to say something kind to someone, because then it becomes about you finding a way to say something nice to someone. Keep it organic! Don't let words stay unspoken if they could lift someone up. You never know what they might do for someone. I will never forget those beautiful and honest words spoken on the bus.

> *A word fitly spoken is like apples of gold in settings of silver.*
>
> —PROVERBS 25:11

7

Goodbye Seizures

I typically always had seizures coming out of a sleep, so I never had one in public. My mom said they would happen in the early morning hours and often she would be walking in to check on me and find that I was beginning a seizure. She would say my name and I would often respond, but when she asked me to point to where she was, I would reach to a completely different area of the room. I often would lose control of my bodily functions and so my mom had to place me on my side so that I would not aspirate my vomit. When I came out of it, I would find myself being put in a warm tub to rinse off the result of losing control of my body. I had them at least once a month and they often lasted as long as 25 minutes. When they were bad enough, my parents had to call the paramedics to check my vitals, which happened at least every other month. Out of the six to eight times a year the paramedics would come to the house, at least four or five times I would end up being taken on an ambulance ride to the hospital. This pattern continued for four years.

I'd always feel exhausted afterward. My mom would have me stay home from school to rest. Thankfully, as a little girl who loved school, it was a breeze for me to catch up on missed assignments. My mom would make me a temporary bed on the living room couch with the softest blankets, and I'd sit and watch Anne of Green Gables. It was the perfect choice for a day like that, because the two-part movie had four VHS tapes to watch through. Although I wondered what fun activity I might be missing at school that day, I was satisfied to watch the continual school house crush between Anne Shirley and Gilbert Blythe play out.

I was on a daily medication called Tegretol in hopes of curbing my seizures. I still remember the spicy taste on my tongue from the so-called "cherry flavored" tablet. I hated taking them.

When I was 8 years old, one night after a Wednesday Bible study, my mom and I went into a little side room and asked some pastors, whose faces I knew very well, to pray for me to be healed from seizures. My parents knew it could go one of two ways: I would keep having seizures, or if it was the Lord's will, they would cease. It wasn't anything crazy, just a small group praying for a miracle. In that moment of prayer I didn't feel anything change or have any kind of sensation. We simply left with hope. Then we waited.

We waited a few weeks and were mildly optimistic when no seizure occurred. My parents finally asked the doctor if they could take me off my seizure medication. They didn't want to seem like some crazy religious parents that didn't believe in science or medication, but they truly believed I had been healed.

To their surprise, the doctor told them they could take me off the medication entirely and see what happened. He said the worst thing that could happen would be that I would start having them more frequently, and I would just have to go back on the medication. I completely went off the medication and the wait began again, this time with more vigilance.

I never had another seizure.

My parents wisely kept one detail from me that the doctor had told them. He said that it was possible that my seizures could go dormant for a while and return when I entered puberty. They never told me about that chance until I was well into my 20s. I'm so thankful for their decision to keep that knowledge from me at the time. It would have made my adolescence something to fear rather than look forward to. I am forever grateful they held that secret for me.

I'm now 34 and have had 26 years of no seizures with no medication to prevent them. I can say with great assurance I was healed from them.

> *Then Jesus answered and said to her, "O woman, great is your faith! Let it be to you as you desire." And her daughter was healed from that very hour.*
> —MATTHEW 15:28

8

David and Goliath

My family's house on Harmony Drive felt like a house out of the movies. We had the corner house with a long driveway and built-in basketball hoop at the top. We had tons of neighborhood kids who would flock to our yard to rollerblade down the driveway or use the epic bike jump that my inventor dad built. I never used it, but I was happy riding my little burnt orange BMX bike around. I wasn't into BMXing. The reason I preferred BMX bikes was because they were closer to the ground, which made me feel more comfortable if I did need to stop myself when I felt off balance. It was a pretty sick bike though. All the biking kids thought it was amazing!

Our yard was always bustling with different activities. Whether we were playing HORSE at the hoop or nighttime hide-and-go-seek, we were always having fun!

My little brother, David, was my constant companion. Since he was five years younger, he was basically my live baby doll until he was old enough to become a fun playmate.

One sunny California day, I was out in the front yard playing around, and 6-year-old David and the kid from two doors down were playing with action figures. The neighbor boy was not just a little big for his age—he was tall and thick, and his dad was probably 6'5". The boy stopped mid-play and said without a thought, "Why does your sister walk so funny?"

In an instant, the previously chill and relaxed David ran, jumped, and tackled the boy to the ground. Even though the boy was twice his size, David was not afraid. In a strong voice, he said, "It's because she has cerebral palsy, that's why!"

That kid jumped up and ran home crying with his hands flailing at his sides. I loved David for it and I still do, though I don't think physical altercations are the answer to rude questions. It wasn't the tackle that made me appreciate my brave little brother; it was the fact that he was worried more about defending my honor than whether he could actually take on the behemoth kid. David dusted himself off and continued his day, like he hadn't done anything special. But that's just who he is, even to this day. He will fight me tooth and nail in a debate, but pull me tightly into a hug after it's all over.

When you have a disability, you know that there will always be people who say ignorant things, whether from inexperience or just carelessness. But it's refreshing to have people in your corner who won't let them get away with it. David didn't have to defend me in that moment, he could have kept playing and no one would have blamed him for it. He was only 6 years old, but instead of being a bystander, he did something.

It seems like people in our society are so worried about what to say or not say. Just have compassion! Your little act of courage may bring some peace to someone who always has to be brave.

> *Then David said to Saul, "Let no man's heart fail because of him; your servant will go and fight with this Philistine."*
>
> —1 Samuel 17:32

9

Little Tribulations

The Seven-Hour Ponytail

As a teenager, you want nothing more than to do things independently. At 13 years old, I couldn't even put my own hair in a ponytail. I was fed up. I watched other girls in my classes swoop their hair up in one swift movement, and I was awed at how smooth the ponytail came out. I would look in amazement and think, "How can they do that so easily?"

One day I decided I wouldn't leave my bathroom until I could figure out a way to put my hair in a ponytail. I tried so many different ways. Each time, one side would come out okay, but there would be a huge bump of hair sticking out on the other side. Or I would manage to get most of the hair up and realize there was still a huge chunk left at the back. Oh, the frustration!

I spent seven hours in front of that bathroom mirror. During those long hours, I somehow figured out how to tie up a ponytail with only one hand. I got all my hair in one tight bunch, twisted it so the hair would stay together and swept it under my chin and held it there while my right hand tied it up at the top. I couldn't believe it actually worked!

By the time I left that bathroom, I was dehydrated and famished and my left hand ached horribly from all the contorting, but I couldn't have felt better. I walked out beaming. I had completed the mission. My hair was in a ponytail.

My disability at times has provided me with opportunities to succeed, even if I'm the only one cheering myself on at the moment. It may seem small to someone looking in, but when you can gain a new independence in even the simplest skill, it's a beautiful thing.

Flip-Flops and High Heels

Where I grew up in Southern California, flip-flops are worn all year long. I would walk through Pacific Sun Wear and eye the flip-flops, wishing I could just slip on a pair and walk around with ease. But when I did try to wear them, on a brave and rare occasion, I instantly regretted it. My left foot would slip and the flip-flop would fall right off. It may not seem like that big of a deal, but at the time, sandals with backs were not cute or fashionable for a teenager to wear.

Ironically, my husband cannot wear flip-flops either, but for a completely different reason. Both of his feet have a couple toes that are webbed, so it makes it basically impossible for him to wear them. On one of our first dates, as I was telling him about some of the little hardships that came with my cerebral palsy, I mentioned the flip-flop issue and he smiled and said that he couldn't wear them either. It's funny how small connections can add so much to a relationship. If you ever bump into us on a beach vacation, we're bound to be wearing sandals with straps.

While I may not have been able to wear flip-flops, I learned that wearing high heels made it easier for me to walk. Now let's be real—I'm not talking stilettos. Those don't help anyone walk easier. But two or three inch heels or wedges are great for me. In many cases when I wore high heels I felt freed from the constant reminder that my heel was not going down as I walked. In the long run, I know heels are probably not the best shoe choice to keep my leg stretched properly, but every now and then it's so nice to walk around and not feel frustrated with my imperfect gait.

When looking down at someone's shoes, you may never know the little tribulations they may walk through each day. Whether they are someone with or without a disability, everyone has to endure hardship from time to time. It is what we do with the hardship that makes us who we are.

> *...we also glory in tribulations, knowing that tribulation produces perseverance; and perseverance, character; and character, hope.*
> —ROMANS 5:3-4

10

Shannan

Shannan never treated me like her little sister with cerebral palsy. We are seven and a half years apart in age and five inches apart in height. We couldn't be any more different in personality. I am the imaginative type who would love to live in the Beauty and the Beast castle library if I could, while sipping from a chipped teacup filled with a cozy latte and writing feverishly about my next idea. She on the other hand is a determined businesswoman who could achieve any professional goal she set her mind on. She also has a bizarre talent of being able to pick something off of a rack in a clothing store and know it'll look amazing on you. And although we have so many differences, we do agree on the stuff that matters—like the best type of music (hip hop) and the best candy (Good and Plenty).

She was what every good sister should be: someone to challenge you. She never gave me an excuse to not do something simply because I had cerebral palsy. She was compassionate, though, and would fight tigers for me if necessary, but she never gave me an out just because I had CP. When I was little, I would try to act tough during a sisterly feud and say, "You widdle, widdle, widdle," and then trail off.

She would squint at me and say, "What, Amy? What am I?"

Then I would back down, like any smart little sister would, and respond with a drawn out, "Nothing . . ."

When I was 10 years old and she was 17, I was already her height and trying to steal her cute T-shirts and sweaters from her closet. To this day when I smell a pear-scented lotion or perfume I think of her. I can imagine standing there looking at her getting ready to go out with friends. That pear aroma gave her an air of being more mature.

She took me to my first concert, N'Sync, in 1999. We got to go backstage, because she knew someone who worked at the Universal City Walk. I bumped into the Olsen twins walking through the crowd and took a picture with Topanga from Boy Meets World. She finished the night by taking me to IHOP for a chocolate shake and then back to her little house for a sister sleepover. I can still remember picturing her white down comforter and how cozy I felt. I don't think I thought about my cerebral palsy one time that day.

To this day, Shannan and I are still as different as two sisters can be. Our dreams and ambitions lie on opposite sides of the spectrum. However, I can picture us waving to each other from either side, hoping the best for the other.

> *But as God has distributed to each one, as the Lord has*
> *called each one, so let him walk . . .*
> —1 Corinthians 7:17

11

Never a Burden

I never felt like I was a burden to my mom. Somehow throughout my entire life she never made me feel like I was an obstacle she had to overcome. I know that there had to be moments where she felt weak and didn't know what to do. She was given so many options by doctors and orthopedic brace makers and physical therapists and occupational therapists, it must have been overwhelming. Somehow she navigated through it all and never made me feel like a burden.

I shouldn't have been recommended for intensive therapy because technically my disability was too mild. I would have to stand before a board who would deem me worthy of physical therapy in order to qualify. The doctors warned my mom that it was very possible I would not pass to receive services at the California Regional Center. However, my mom pushed forward anyway. As a toddler, I walked back and forth in front of the board's decision-makers, and they decided in my favor.

After that, my mom took me to physical therapy three times a week. I think perhaps that is when I gained my love for long car drives. Though I don't remember all the details, I can imagine those car drives were filled with endless stories told by me and sing-alongs with my mom.

Being a mom myself now, I understand wanting to do anything to help my precious babies. However, I don't have a child with a disability so I don't really know what that feels like. I won't try to, either. I know God will equip me for whatever His plan for my life is. If one of my children were disabled, they would be just as precious in my sight, and I'd know a little of what they were going through since I grew up with a disability myself. However, we all have obstacles we must face, whether it's a disability, a bad temper, a shy demeanor, or something else.

As a parent, it's a beautiful thing to observe these adorable developing people with their own unique personalities and physiques. I can sit and just watch my two daughters play. My oldest, Ruby, is currently 3 years old and Ava is just around the corner from turning 2! They're only 18 months apart and yet they couldn't be more different, from eye color to temperament, they are truly unique. When I look at my sweet babies, I want them to accomplish anything they set their minds to. I will being cheering them on their whole lives, no matter what obstacles they face.

I am forever grateful for my mom's diligence and grace throughout my life. She is my advocate and my cheerleader. As a mom myself, I have gained a new appreciation for all she did for me. I love her so much. I understand now how important it is for disabled children to have parents like her, who are loving and supportive no matter what, willing to do whatever is necessary, and who never make their children or their children's disabilities feel like a burden.

> *Strength and honor are her clothing; she shall rejoice in time to come.*
>
> —PROVERBS 31:25

12

Mildly Disabled

As a little girl, while I sat with my mom in the waiting room to see a neurologist or a physical therapist, often the mothers of the other children in the room would look at me questioningly, wondering why I was there. I don't blame them at all. I sat there in the chair looking rather "normal"—whatever that means—while other children might have their heads strapped back in wheelchairs or moved their limbs uncontrollably.

It was hard not to feel a sense of guilt at times. I had the same diagnosis as they did, yet I lived a relatively normal and independent life. Most people don't know that every step I take, I can feel that my heel isn't going down the way it should. I can't step down onto the first step of an escalator without feeling a moment of pure terror.

Having mild cerebral palsy means people often tell me they can barely even tell that I have cerebral palsy or that if I hadn't told them, they would never have even known that I had cerebral palsy. What is the appropriate response to those comments? "Thank you"? "Yes, I'm glad I'm not a little bit more disabled"? "If you had been able see my disability, would you have thought something different about me"? There's nothing inherently wrong with these comments. I know people are just reassuring me that I don't stick out too much with my disability. But it is interesting to see how people respond to hearing or noticing that I am disabled, when it is not always immediately apparent.

I teeter on a line of living in the land of the able and the disabled. I don't mean this in a self-pitying way at all. I am thankful that I have mild cerebral palsy. No one would wish to have a more severe case of whatever disability they possess. I'm thankful I can get up in the morning, make coffee for my husband and myself, and take care of my two daughters. And before I became a stay-at-home mom, I was glad I could get up and prepare to teach 30 students in a classroom. I know that if my disability had been more severe, some of those things would not have been possible.

But there are aspects of my life that are different from someone without a disability. Having mild cerebral palsy means that you think about things that other people wouldn't have to worry about. For example, what activity does your group of friends have planned and is it something that you're going to enjoy? Or is it something you'll hate the entire time because you can't do it well or at all? Mountain biking? Never going to happen! But leisurely biking down a beach path on a cruiser bicycle with a flower basket on the front is a very different story.

I can ride a bike, but I don't want to go down a dirt path that shakes my bike back-and-forth and makes me feel like I'm going to fall. One guy took me mountain biking on a first date. And yes, I fell multiple times. In my hard-headedness I thought, "I'm going do it. I can do this!" No, I couldn't do it. In his defense, I actually think he was trying to prove to me that he didn't think any differently of me even though I had cerebral palsy. On the other hand, on my first date with my husband, he took me out to sushi and a movie and then ended it with stroll through the park. He knew me, without even knowing me yet.

Being mildly disabled has definitely given me a unique perspective on life. I think more than anything it has shown me that you never know what someone is silently enduring. The man sitting in the car next to you at a stoplight might be nervous about presenting a demonstration on a new product because he stutters when he gets anxious. Perhaps the irritable lady behind the counter at the bank can't afford to pay her rent. Or the little girl who doesn't want to walk up to the board to show her math work doesn't want people staring at her while she limps to the front of the classroom. You never know what someone is going through. Understanding this on a deeply personal level helps me have compassion and patience even when it doesn't come easy.

> *If I say, "My foot slips," Your mercy, O Lord, will hold me up.*
>
> —Psalm 94:18

.

13

Dancing and Typing

Before we were born my mom watched a documentary about how some African women pat their babies' chest to the beat of music so that they develop a sense of rhythm. My mom is an incredible dancer and so she wanted all of her children to have a good sense of rhythm if possible. As fate would have it, my sister, my brother, and I all know how to dance. Even with cerebral palsy, I still know how to move rather well. In fact, I was the girl in the middle of the circle at school dances, "battling" other girls, as we called it.

Dancing is the only activity that makes me not even think about my cerebral palsy. One particularity about my CP is that it makes my left side do what my right side is doing. It's called crossover. Normally it is incredibly annoying, but when it comes to dancing it's actually very helpful. Don't get me wrong, following some intricate hip hop choreography would not be easy, but for most dancing, it's helpful. For example, when I make a fist with my right hand, my left hand automatically does it, unless I mentally tell it not to, which usually doesn't work super well, so I end up sitting on my hand or putting my hand flat on a surface to help keep it from moving. When it comes to dancing, my left hand mimicking my right actually makes dancing more easy and fun.

It is the crossover that makes typing on a computer a real challenge, and so I type one-handed. I've actually gotten very fast at it. It was a battle through high school, because more and more papers had to be typed, so I just figured out a way to do it. I will often use my left hand to push tab or some other outlying button, but all the other keys are under the mercy of my speedy right hand.

When I started teaching, coworkers and students would watch me type and they were floored that I could type as fast as I could with one hand. Students would come up while I was working on a computer and ask me why I typed with one hand. Fortunately for my fourth graders, they were learning home row in computer class, which of course is the most efficient way to type. I told them, "You learn home row if you can, because it's the best way to do it if you're able! I can't type with my left hand, so I've got to do it this way."

Their sweet little 10-year-old faces would look back at me and smile and then I would see them walk over to some other student and excitedly say, "Have you seen how Miss Hirsch types?!"

The typical responses were, "Yeah, she types with one hand, you didn't know that?" Or "No way!" Then another student would run up to me to check the accuracy of the other student's statement.

It's amazing how sometimes my cerebral palsy can seem like such a burden and yet it has made me persevere in so many small things.

I can do all things through Christ who strengthens me.
—PHILIPPIANS 4:13

14

Stretching

Stretching, as we all know, is so good for the body whether you have a disability or not. But when you have to stretch so that you walk semi-normal, it's the most irritating and troublesome activity. It is laborious and only rewarding in the long run. If you have CP, you don't feel super great after you stretch. You may feel a tiny bit better, but to feel a difference from stretching, you have to stretch day after day.

Do I stretch every day? No!

Should I? Yes!

From third grade until the end of fourth grade, I wore a leg brace daily. The intention of the brace was to keep my heel down and stretch out my calf muscle as I walk. It was the mid-90s, so thankfully mine was made out of a light plastic, not one of the metal ones depicted in older movies. But until you have had to wear a brace yourself, you really can't understand the little frustrations that come with it. Often my brace would click as I walked. So not only did I walk with a limp, but I got to hear a constant clicking reminding me I wasn't walking well.

I also had to buy shoes wide enough to adequately house my brace, so shoe choices were not great. I remember trying on shoes and the only ones that worked with the brace were a pair of hideous blue tennis shoes with wide white shoe laces. I hated them so much, but they were the best option. I know it broke my mom's heart, because she knew that I didn't like them either, but we didn't have any other choice.

Later on, I also wore a night brace that was supposed to help stretch my leg at night. I would change into my pajamas and put a knee-high sock on and strap my leg in. That brace didn't last long because in the middle of the night I would have to rip the four Velcro straps open and release my leg to keep it from feeling like it was going to pull my tendon apart.

The Lord stretching me in my spiritual walk is so similar; I want it and I know how amazing it is for my life, but it can take a long time for me to see the difference. God has stretched me in ways I would never have imagined!

Whenever I think of being stretched not only physically but spiritually, I think of my mission trip to Heidelberg, Germany. I had just turned 18 years old and the church I was going to at the time, called Calvary Chapel Chino Hills, announced on a Sunday morning they were looking for a team of people to go share the gospel in the beautiful European college town. I knew God was tugging on my heart to go.

When I went to the first meeting I was excited, but the thing I was most intimidated by was the amount of walking I would be doing. Would my left side be able to keep up? I pushed the thought aside and said to myself, "If I'm meant to go, the Lord will equip me." My mom wasn't originally going to go, but they called her last minute to see if she could join the team. It was fun to have her with me and it brought me some comfort to know she would be there for me if I was exhausted.

When we eventually arrived in Heidelberg, I was instantly awestruck by its incredible sights. Even before the plane landed, all I saw underneath us was lush forest. We stayed in a hostel and roomed with other members of our group. It was interesting to wake up to the sound of German being spoken over the loud speaker to inform us about breakfast time. I knew a bit of German from taking a class my freshman year of high school, but not enough to decipher the muffled announcements. We learned a few phrases, such as "Jeshua liebt dich," which means "Jesus loves you."

I was already being stretched by being in a country where I knew little of the mother tongue, and to top it off, I was going to most likely being talking to college intellectuals about Jesus, all the while hoping that the shoes I had would carry my feet down old cobblestone paths without giving me too much pain. I knew I was in for a challenge, but I also knew I served an incredible God who for some reason wanted me on this trip.

I spoke to so many people from different walks of life. Once, I sat on the grass in the park across from three college students who were so confident in their atheist views. They had sat near some music our group was playing and I approached them along with another girl from our group. We didn't have a translator with us, but luckily they spoke English well. Right away, they asked us what brought us to their little town by the river, and we explained that we came to talk to people about Jesus. They smiled, as if to say, "That's sweet," but immediately started discussing all they knew about a world that didn't need God to exist.

One of the translators, a college-aged guy from Munich, came over to help us out with some of the language barriers when the conversation got deeper. It was so neat to watch him talk to them with such love, hoping they would see the truth in what we were saying. I told them that I believed there was a God and He had me travel across the globe, perhaps only to have this one conversation and tell them how much He loves them. I don't know what came of those three guys or whether they have found Jesus for themselves yet, but by the end of the conversation, they shook our hands and thanked us for the intriguing conversation.

One night, I crashed on my bottom bunk after a long day of constant walking. My mom saw webs in the corner above my bed and was worried there might be spiders. But I was so exhausted from the day, I'll never forget what I said to her: "God can make the spiders stay in their webs. I'm going to bed, I'm tired." Only on a trip like that could I have knowingly went to bed with webs hanging in the corner above my feet. I still can't believe I did that.

When we got back from the trip, Jack, the pastor at Calvary Chapel Chino Hills, asked if some of the team would speak at the Wednesday night Bible study about our experiences in Heidelberg. They wanted me to be one of the people to share, not only because of my age, but because of the physical obstacles that accompanied me on the trip. I stood in front of the large congregation, talking about my time there. I explained what God had done and how He used my cerebral palsy to reach people in Germany and gave me the strength to physically endure it each day.

I remember a mom coming up to me afterwards. She told me she was so excited to hear me talking about going on a trip like that while having my disability. She explained to me that she had a son who was disabled and it encouraged her to hear how God was able to use my disability. That following Sunday, I sat down and talked with the little boy. It was a short conversation, he was animated and spoke excitedly about something he had seen earlier. I'll never forget the look on his mom's face. She was so relieved to see a teenage girl with a disability who was still able to do big things.

God stretches me in ways I could never have imagined before they happened. It is amazing to think that, in a world constantly striving for perfection, there is a God who can equip even the most unexpected person to accomplish the most interesting purpose.

> *"My grace is sufficient for you, for My strength is made perfect in weakness. Therefore most gladly I will rather boast in my infirmities, that the power of Christ may rest upon me. Therefore I take pleasure in infirmities, in reproaches, in needs, in persecutions, in distresses, for Christ's sake. For when I am weak, then I am strong."*
> —2 CORINTHIANS 12:9-10

15

Creative Therapies

When I was 2 years old, my mom heard about a local woman named Pat Morris who did equestrian therapy for children with many different disabilities. When I first started the therapy, I was placed in a little seat that resembled a small car seat that went on top of the horse's saddle. Even now when I smell something similar to the scent of a corral dampened by the early morning air, it brings me joy. I loved being with the horses. I rode a horse named Softy for years.

As I got a little older, I did exercises to help strengthen my left side. I was constantly reminded to keep my heels down in the stirrup. It's a skill that all riders need to remember, but it was great therapy to force my left side to stay down during the entirety of the ride.

Often one of the people helping out would lead my horse by rope while I sat on the saddle with both arms out as straight as possible to strengthen my core. They would increase the speed of the horse just a bit and encourage me to sit up straight in the saddle, since I naturally lean to one side.

Like in many other instances when I was in a group setting with other disabled children, I was one of very few that appeared to be pretty able-bodied. Most of the other children were very severely disabled and could barely stay on top of the horse without assistance. In those moments, I thought of how brave those children were. I felt privileged to be able to throw my leg over the back of the horse with a little help and hold the reins independently. Those moments made me grateful for what ability I did have.

I continued equestrian therapy until I was around 7 years old, when we moved to a different city. However, by some crazy turn of events, Pat moved her therapy lessons right up the road from my house about a year later. I rode again with her for another two years. I'm thankful I got to experience such a unique type of therapy from a young age. I greatly appreciated her dedication to holding those therapy sessions every Saturday morning for children who wouldn't have had the opportunity to ride otherwise.

In my early 20s, I started seeing a personal trainer. I wanted to get more fit, but I also needed direction on how to help bring my left shoulder back, because it often likes to lean forward. I also wanted help stretching out my left calf to improve my gait. Brian, my personal trainer, was not a physical therapist, but he had many certifications in sports medicine and strength and conditioning. When he found out I had cerebral palsy, he was excited by the challenge, which made me excited too. Instead of being intimidated to train someone with a disability, he welcomed it and even did side research to tailor my sessions to my ability.

Brian had me try difficult exercises to see where my limitations were and pushed me just enough to help me to improve. He was the only real "coach" I've ever had. I never desired to play in organized sports as a kid, so it was fun to experience what it felt like to be pushed by someone to achieve goals in fitness. In just a few months he was able to help my shoulder pull back naturally, and my core strength improved dramatically, which helped me walk more smoothly.

Brian became like a big brother to me. He repeated phrases that still stick with me, like, "Amy, it doesn't matter what your day was like. Just do one thing better today." He showed me how strong I could get if I put my mind to it.

Although I've had some unique therapy treatments, the most mystifying I have ever experienced has been changing a squirming baby's diaper. Both of my girls have provided me with a newfound challenging therapy for my left hand. My sweet little baby transforms into an energetic baby alligator flopping back and forth as I, Mommy Dundee, try to manage to take off the dirty diaper and replace it with a fresh one.

The irony of my babies turning into a type of therapy for me is that my mom used to buy me baby dolls and clothes with Velcro and buttons so that I would have to use both my left hand and right hand to put clothes on my dolls. Now I have real life babies who force me to use my left hand in a way I've never had to before.

Physical therapy can come in so many shapes and sizes. Sometimes it can be a set time and place, but it can also be a simple daily task. I either have to move it or lose it, so I try to see a difficult physical obstacle as a way to challenge myself. Sometimes I have to tap out from exhaustion, but at least I tried.

> *When you walk, your steps will not be hindered, and*
> *when you run, you will not stumble.*
> —Proverbs 4:12

16

Accepting Imperfections

Recorded on VHS on my family's giant camcorder is a video of a Christmas program at church composed of a bunch of elementary kids singing Christmas songs and little boys and girls dressed up as angels and shepherds giving monologues about the true meaning of Christmas. I have such fond memories of that program, although you may not believe it if you saw the footage of me in the crowd of children. For most of the video, I just raised my eyebrows and pursed my lips in nervousness. The VHS tape also contained footage of my brother's second birthday.

As a teenager I stumbled across the tape and was so excited to watch it. I was still able to because we had a DVD and VHS combo player. Yeah—we were pretty cutting edge. I watched the birthday portion and then the Christmas program popped onto the screen. I fast forwarded through some of the songs and what was shown next made my heart drop.

Growing up in a time where videos were not as easily taken, I didn't see myself on camera a lot. The part that struck me was when a little girl was walking down the stage after the group had been released. She had a gold ribbon in her hair and a beautiful red velvet holiday dress. She walked with her left arm lifted high near her chest and her left leg struggled to keep up as she walked carefully down the stage steps. I sat there in disbelief. I couldn't believe that I actually looked like that when I walked.

That image was etched in my memory from that day on. So when I felt myself walking poorly from exhaustion, I would wonder if that was what I looked like to onlookers. I'm sure that many teenage girls desire to carry themselves beautifully. When watching a movie, I often catch myself admiring the gorgeous dress the actress has on and how she carries herself across the room. I knew deep down that even if I was adorned in such a beautiful outfit, my walk would never match hers.

When I was around 14 years old, I saw a new neurologist for a checkup. I had just received a shoe insert that the orthopedic brace makers had suggested for my left shoe in another attempt to correct my gait. Unfortunately, when I walked with it in my shoes, it often caused my left heel to slip out of the back of my shoe, causing even more frustration. I pulled it out of my shoe to show the new doctor and he looked straight at me and said one of the most heart-piercing but honest things I had ever heard from a doctor: "If you feel like this insert helps your walk, that's great! However, you need to know something. You have cerebral palsy, so you're going to walk with a limp."

That statement made me so mad for a moment. But when it actually had time to sink in, it gave me a new confidence. I had spent so much time up until then figuring out a way to improve my gait.

I am by no means saying that braces are not beneficial in aiding millions of people with physical disabilities. The question that I came to ask that day was, "Why am I wearing this particular insert? Is it going to improve my gait?" And the answer was no. I would always walk with a limp. And at 34 years old, I still do. And when I'm 101, I will as well. I've accepted that. The acceptance of my imperfect gait has made me able to walk with confidence.

Thank goodness that when I sometimes get stuck in my self-centered brain, the Lord reminds me that He formed me just as He planned, and I accept the fact that I have a limp. A limp that has struck up so many conversations about how God has done amazing things in my life. A limp that reminds me though my walk is imperfect, the God who designed it had the perfect plan for using it.

> *But those who wait on the Lord shall renew their strength;*
> *they shall mount up with wings like eagles, they shall run*
> *and not be weary, they shall walk and not faint.*
> —Isaiah 40:31

17

The Special Education Professor

During my junior year of college, before I started student teaching, I attended a class to educate future teachers about inclusion for special needs in the classroom. During a lecture, the professor used a PowerPoint to explain some of the attributes of different types of disabilities we may encounter as teachers. When the slide for cerebral palsy popped up, I was interested to see how he would explain it.

To my surprise, unlike he'd done for any of the other disabilities, he took it upon himself to impersonate a person with CP. My heart began to pound loudly in my chest. He put his arm to his chest with his wrist hanging limply, and he deformed his mouth so that he spoke with an impediment. He finished his charade and seemed quite pleased with the job he had done.

I took a deep breath and raised my hand.

"Yes?" he asked.

And then I began. I told him how I thought that it was important to realize that not all students who come into our classrooms will have severe cases of these disabilities, and in fact you might not even know that a student has one until you are informed.

He replied, "Yes, that's true. What makes you so passionate about it?"

"Well, because I have cerebral palsy and I don't think I look like what you portrayed."

I think the air was sucked out of the classroom by all the gasps. I have to admit I've never seen someone's jaw drop quite as severely as his did.

Rather than apologizing, he started backpedaling. He even had the audacity to say that I must have had a lot of physical therapy, because he could barely tell that I had it. I realized that no matter how many years he had studied and taught special education, somewhere along the way he'd lost his compassion. Perhaps he had even forgotten why he chose special education for his field of study.

This professor and the university shall remain nameless. It's not my intention to call him out. I only write this experience to show that inclusion in the classroom does not only mean you should adjust your instruction to meet the needs of all types of students, but also to lead by example and teach students that they never know what a classmate may silently endure.

If we teach empathy, inclusion will come naturally in both our classrooms and homes.

> *But You, Oh Lord, are a God full of compassion, and*
> *gracious, longsuffering and abundant in mercy and truth.*
> —Psalm 86:15

18

My Quiet Supporter

On the way back from a trip that my family took when I was a baby, I began crying and didn't stop for almost the entire three hours it took to get home. It was on that noisy car drive that my dad discovered a way to soothe my tears. He was eventually able to lull me to sleep by reaching into the backseat and rubbing his thumb in the middle of my left palm, my hand with the CP. It wasn't just a one-time fix, and he used the comforting tactic on many occasions to come.

My dad is a man of few words. He is passionate about many things, but he is content to sit and listen instead of dominating the discussion. He didn't just teach me the typical dad lessons like changing a tire. I received what I would consider a very well-rounded upbringing. I was shown which webs housed which spiders. I was taught that black widows were not our friends, but jumping spiders were. To this day I still hesitate to kill a jumping spider, because I hear his words in my mind saying, "Jumping spiders won't bother you. They're cool little guys that eat the more dangerous spiders." I learned to recognize the smell of epoxy resin when walking into the garage to see him working on his custom cars.

My favorite activity with my dad was watching him paint. All the little colorful tubes would come out and I loved peeling the dried paint from the plastic palettes—it was so satisfying. It was as if time slowed down when I did these types of activities with him. My dad taught me how to sit and ponder. He is probably much to thank for my interest in writing. He showed me by his example to stop and consider things.

My dad has been such a steady force in my life. I knew he was always there for me, quietly cheering me on. He was one of the big decision makers in my medical journey, even though he was often behind the scenes. He and my mom would discuss what to do before or after a doctor's appointment. They discussed multiple options that came up at different phases of my life. I know they often prayed for guidance in deciding what direction to go.

I remember lying on the floor with all my stuffed animals and dolls at the foot of his drawing table and looking up as I watched him work. Whether he was completing his shop drawing for a big sky-rise in Los Angeles or sketching a new design for an invention, he was always creating. The best part was I could interrupt him at any time to tell him a story or share the name I decided on for a new doll. He would just listen and nod. He listened to me in such a way that I knew my words had value. As a parent myself, I know how easy it is to listen but not truly hear what your child is saying. My dad truly heard me. Whether you have a disability or not, to be truly heard is one of the most precious things in life.

I still call my dad on a regular basis to tell him about a headline I read or a spider I spotted recently. When I hear the phrase "Jack-of-all-trades," I sometimes think it should instead be "Jeff-of-all-trades," after my dad. I'm not quite sure there is anything he doesn't know how to do or couldn't learn if he tried.

The two of us are so different in personality, but we are also two artists—me with my pen and he with his paintbrush and hammer. His life has taught me that although I deal with obstacles from my cerebral palsy at times, God has given me a gift to express myself with words, and writing them down gives those words a new purpose.

> *How precious also are Your thoughts to me, O God! How great is the sum of them!*
>
> —Psalm 139:17

19

Someone to Hold My Hand

When I met my husband, Sean, the first thing I noticed was the way he took my hand. He grabbed my hand so sweetly in our first hand-shake, it instantly put me at ease. He looked me in eyes and raised his eyebrows and said, "Well, hello." Then he held my hand for a moment more. We had been set up by a mutual friend and liked each other from the start. Our conversation flowed effortlessly. Just being around Sean made me feel at peace.

On our second date, after dinner, we went to a movie and he sat on my left side. I thought, "He's going to hold my left hand." There was something special about it. He took my hand as the movie was about to begin. My fingers didn't slide so easily into his as my right hand had on the date before. I leaned over and whispered, "This is my left hand. I have to try to rearrange my fingers." His reaction was so sweet. He sat there with his palm laid open and watched carefully as I positioned each finger. I felt so safe with my hand clutched in his that night. He had no idea at the time what that moment meant to me.

On our fourth date, we walked a long distance in the park and he wanted to walk on my left side so that he could shield me from possible oncoming traffic. As he took my hand, we once again had to figure out how I could keep my grasp without constant struggle. We tried gripping a couple different ways and laughed as we could not get it quite right. Then finally I grasped onto his big, manly thumb, and it was perfect. We both looked down and he said with a smile, "That works!" Even though no onlooker would have noticed, we knew we had conquered something great. It's as if the Lord said, "Yes, you can take her hand."

Sean helps me with the little things. He cuts my steak into pieces when my left hand doesn't quite have the energy to do it. He takes my hand to help me up an uneven hill. When we're sitting on the couch watching TV, he'll put his foot under my left foot to help push my toes back to relieve my tight left calf that had helped in aiding a limping leg all day. He doesn't think he's doing me any great favor, he just does these things. I love him for that! He is so thoughtful without even thinking about it.

He finds joy in the little successes I have when dealing with my cerebral palsy on a daily basis. I feel that has to be a must if you are in a relationship with someone with a disability. I can't imagine not having that kind of support from him. For example, if I attempt to pick something small up with my left hand and am successful in my attempt, I'll look and ask if he saw what I just did. If he happened to catch a glimpse of it, he'll respond with something like, "Whoa, look at you!" The delight in his eyes speaks so much louder than his words.

When thinking about doing something new or going on an adventure, he often will overestimate my ability and allow me to set my own limitations. He always wants to give me the opportunity to try something and often it is something I wouldn't have tried on my own if he wasn't there with me. Whether it's camping in the middle of nowhere or hiking up a hill of snow to sled down, he has shown me that I can do so much more than I ever realized.

Sean challenges me in the most beautiful way. He holds my hand through the hard stuff, but when I succeed in doing something on my own, he applauds me and cheers me on to go further. He has a reassuring, understated confidence about him. I love supporting him in his life pursuit of building and customizing beautiful experimental aircraft. While I know he cherishes my support, he doesn't allow me to forget my own dreams. We balance each other out well. I am the optimistic "anything is possible" girl and he is the level-headed "hope for the best, expect the worst" guy. He keeps me grounded while I help him dream.

Who knew that a blind date set up by a friend would flourish into something this amazing? God brought me someone who doesn't love me *despite* my cerebral palsy, but instead embraces all of me and loves me deeply. And when my hands show wrinkles and veins, I'm glad I will be able to look down and see his well-worn hand still holding mine.

> *Love suffers long and is kind; love does not envy; love does not parade itself, is not puffed up ...*
> —1 Corinthians 13:4

20

Our Precious Gem

Finding out I was pregnant with Ruby was one of the most exciting experiences of my life. Once we found out we were having a girl, the bows and dresses came flooding in. I'd decided years before that if I ever had a girl, her name would be Ruby. I always thought it would be so sweet to think of her as a gem. Thankfully, my husband liked the name too.

For the most part, my body handled pregnancy quite well. It was only in the last four weeks that I could barely walk. You might think that isn't so bad for 36 weeks pregnant, but try being 36 weeks pregnant and having a limp. Not so fun, but so worth it. I was amazed at times myself to see how my body coped and adjusted to carry my sweet baby to full term. In fact, she was six days late.

For years, I vowed to never get a handicap parking pass. I told myself that there was absolutely no way I would take a parking spot that somebody worse off than me may need to use. As parenthood often teaches, you must be willing to change, even for things you never thought you'd do before. I finally gave in as the pressure on my tight left leg became worse with the weight of the baby. It not only helped me during the pregnancy, but also when I had to carry the ridiculously heavy baby carrier to the front of the store. I would park right next to the cart return and bring the cart to the side of the car so I could put Ruby's car seat right in. She's now at the age that she can walk beside me and hold my hand while her little sister rides in the seat.

Ruby made me a mother for the first time. Whether you're a person with or without a disability, becoming a parent for the first time is a life-altering event. She showed me that though I may have to do things a little differently with my left side to be able to do all the little daily tasks it takes to be a mom, I can do it.

Ruby is a burst of joy everywhere she goes. People often comment that she's always smiling. She makes people so comfortable around her. She's only 3, but she is a natural hostess. She puts her palm out to point out things that she feels are important for her guests to observe. When her Grammy comes over, she is quick to say hello and point out where Ava, her little sister, is, so that my mom can say hi to her as well. When she meets new children, she instantly makes them her friends and plays with them effortlessly. She is such an incredible example in how she loves so simply. She expects nothing in return for her kind gestures and finds delight in the act itself.

Ruby looks basically like a carbon copy of me as a kid. It's pretty remarkable seeing our pictures side by side at the same ages. I have to admit it is fun having a little mini me. However, she is quite the adventurous type. When I was Ruby's age, I had to be much more calculated in my moves because of my limitations from cerebral palsy. Ruby throws caution to the wind, doing crazy jumps off the couch or whatever strikes her fancy. I am thankful that she gets to live life uninhibited by a disability. However, it's interesting to think that the lessons I learned in perseverance through my cerebral palsy she will learn another way. It's such a beautiful way of looking at life. We are all given different versions of obstacles in life, but we are learning many of the same lessons.

I look at Ruby and see such a beautiful future. Her little eyes take in the world around her with such amazement and delight. She reminds me to look at the little details around me. Whoever thought hearing a bird in the backyard would be bring such happiness? She reminds me continually to find joy in the little things. She truly is a gem and I would keep her in my pocket forever if I could.

> *You will show me the path of life; in Your presence is fullness of joy; at Your right hand are pleasures forevermore.*
>
> —PSALM 16:11

21

Blue-Eyed Cuddle Bug

The second time I became pregnant, Sean and I made a list of potential baby names. When I saw "Ava" on the list, I knew I had to have her. I had to have an Ava. She was meant to be born with that name. When the technician confirmed my suspicion that I was having another girl, I wasn't surprised.

Ava is extraordinary in so many ways. When she was born, her cry sounded like she was saying "mama." I had never heard a baby cry that way before. She peeks out of the stroller at passers-by and her ocean blue eyes catch them completely off guard. She has a way of looking at someone and truly seeing them. She observes her surroundings like she's accumulating as much information as she possibly can. I can't wait to hear her thoughts about the world when she's able to express them clearly.

Ava will often crawl up on the couch and rest her head on Sean or me. She lets a big breath out and lays her head down so purposely. It's as if she is fully taking in the moment.

The meaning of her name is "living" or "breath." There is no doubt in my mind that she won't let life pass her by without taking in deep breaths to appreciate the splendor around her.

Patience doesn't come naturally to Ava. She wants things done quickly, even when she's doing them herself. If pages in a book aren't cooperating with her little hands, she gets frustrated. But she doesn't give up! She makes it happen, huffing and puffing as she does. Ava reminds me that staying frustrated in a situation is fruitless. The more she struggles to get something done, the harder the task becomes. When she finally slows down and tries a different approach, she often experiences success.

Sometimes Ava looks to me for assistance when she can't quite figure out what to do. She trusts that I can help her. It's very much the same as my situation. I could continue to attempt to solve a difficult problem by trying again and again, or I can step back and look at it in a different way. Even better, I can look to the Lord, whom I trust, to lead me in the right direction.

It's amazing to watch the thought process of a growing toddler as she completes what seems to be a simple task. It is only simple to an adult because we have conquered those skills. They have become second nature. But I understand, as someone with a disability, what it feels like to not be able to complete tasks others may view as simple.

My cerebral palsy reminds me that I need to slow down and correct my approach—whether I am trying to open a door with my left hand while holding a baby on my right hip or questioning why I was born with a disability at all. I love Ava so dearly, and I hope to teach her many things as she grows. But I am so thankful for the lessons she teaches me as I raise her.

> *Take My yoke upon you and learn from Me, for I am gentle and lowly in heart, and you will find rest for your souls.*
>
> —Matthew 11:29

22

Who Would I Be Without It?

Who would I be if I didn't have cerebral palsy? It's an interesting question to ask myself. It's scary to think of myself without CP. To see myself without certain limitations, it is almost dreamlike. What would it be like to walk across a street without feeling my gait? To pick up something small with my right hand without feeling my left hand clenching as I do it? I do wonder sometimes—I don't know how someone in my position couldn't.

The one thing I do know for sure is that the Lord allowed me to have cerebral palsy. And I have accepted that. I have examined it and realized it has given me a unique experience. It's given me eyes that can see into a world of disability and on occasion slip unnoticed into the land of the able. My cerebral palsy doesn't define me, but it is a big part of me, and it has played a significant role in who I have become.

Why is anyone born with a certain disability? Why do people get into accidents and then develop disabilities? Even if you're not disabled, perhaps something bothers you about yourself, and you ask yourself a similar question—why am I like this? Physical and emotional burdens can awaken you to things in life that you never would have noticed before.

Everyone has their own set of insecurities. Maybe it's the tone of your voice, the way you laugh, or the way you walk. I think what the Lord has shown me most through my CP is that I don't need to worry about my disability as much as I think I do. Instead, I need to live and breathe and in Henry David Thoreau's words, "suck the marrow out of life."

If all I did was focus on my limitations, I'd never overcome obstacles. Whether it was learning how to put a ponytail in my own hair or type one handed, I walked forward, one step at a time.

So why do I walk this way? Because I was meant to.

While I have relied on God to give me the strength and the confidence I need throughout the day, God was never just my crutch. Whether you have cerebral palsy or you're someone who has life all together, I want you to know that you do need God. Not for the sake of having religion, but because God wants you. He wants to have a relationship with you. He didn't create you to leave you alone, trying to figure out life yourself. What He wants you to do is surrender your life to Him.

Being a Christian is not just about being a good person. It's about finding the truth, because there is only one truth: God loves you and wants to know you. He loved you so much that He sent His Son to die on the cross for your sins so you and I would have the chance to be reconciled to Him.

I had to come to the realization that God allowed me to have cerebral palsy for a reason. And if that reason was just so that you could read these words right now, that would be enough. If you truly desire to know God, He will show Himself to you.

So, to all of you who have asked, "Why do you walk that way?" I must answer with this: God allowed me to have cerebral palsy and I still chose to walk His path. He has blessed me beyond what I could have imagined.

> *"But sanctify the Lord God in your hearts, and always be ready to give a defense to everyone who asks you a reason for the hope that is in you …"*
> —1 Peter 3:15

> *Jesus said to him, "I am the Way, the Truth, and the Life. No one comes to Father except through Me."*
> —John 14:6

Resources

There are many resources out there for and by people with cerebral palsy. Some of the most helpful and inspirational to me have been people who offer encouragement and perspective about their disabilities to help others process what it means to have a disability, and to spread awareness and compassion among the general public.

Jason Benetti is an announcer for the Chicago White Sox who has CP and is known for his catchphrase, "Just say hi." He encourages people not to shy away from those who are different, but to treat them with respect. His series of videos called "Awkward Moments" gives an uplifting perspective on viewing disabilities in society. Interacting with people who have disabilities doesn't have to be difficult if you treat each other with decency and respect. In light, cartoonish short videos, he tells stories of interactions he's had in public when someone notices his disability. In one story, a mother hushed her child when he asked about Jason's disability in a movie theater line. Jason suggests it would have been better for the mother to tell the child to "just say hi." There's no reason to be afraid to interact with people who are unlike yourself. His simple examples of how we can make talking about disabilities less of a taboo are very relatable and create easy lessons to teach children how we can treat everyone with respect.

Gianna Jesson is an incredible inspirational speaker and activist. She survived being aborted and was also diagnosed with cerebral palsy.

Don't let her sweet and gracious appearance deceive you—she is a force to be reckoned with when she speaks before doctors about her unlikely survival. She now lives her life for Christ and is dedicated to being a voice for the unborn. Her story will bring tears to your eyes.

Love That Max is a blog by Ellen Seidman, a mom whose son has cerebral palsy. She writes "to help people better see the ability in disability." Shortly after her first child, Max, was born, he began having seizures, and then a stroke. The blog tells Max's story and relates the struggles Ellen went through as a mother. This is a fantastic resource for parents of children with CP and even other disabilities.

Zachary Fenell is a blogger, author, YouTuber, and speaker with cerebral palsy. He believes in challenging himself and pushing the limits of what is considered possible. He has even completed marathons. He has a number of encouraging resources for individuals with CP.

Credits

To my husband, Sean, for always encouraging me to finish this book.
To my mom and dad, for always listening to my stories.

To Maryanna Young,
Megan Terry,
Heather Goetter,
and the entire team at Aloha Publishing,
for their help in bringing this book to life.

And to all my family and friends
who were there for me on my journey
to complete this book.

About the Author

Amy Cole is a wife, mother, teacher, and now stay-at-home mom. Encouraging parents and teachers is what fuels her passion to pursue her lifelong dream of writing and sharing her story. She was diagnosed with mild hemiplegic cerebral palsy at 10 months old.

Despite the life challenges and daily obstacles her disability may bring, she chooses to live with joy and perseverance, knowing there is a greater plan in place. She has not let it hold her back from becoming a teacher and now a full-time mom, modeling her perspective of hope for both her students and her children. She prays that her story can be a light for people with disabilities as well as for parents of disabled children in the midst of the unknown a heavy medical diagnosis creates.

Amy currently lives in southern Idaho with her husband, Sean, and her two young daughters, Ruby and Ava.

Connect With Me

You can follow me on my journey as an author
on my Instagram page @authoramycole

Feel free to email me at amy.cole717@gmail.com

If you liked this book, please give this book
an Amazon five star review.
It helps other parents and teachers find this book so
it can empower more individuals with CP.
Thank you sincerely for bringing positive change in the world.

Made in the USA
Las Vegas, NV
17 January 2022

41628335R00058